Luong Thanh Tran / Katarina Dulkova
The Western Tendency to outsource Problems

AF003941

Review of Essential Economic Aspects

Volume 1

# The Western Tendency to outsource Problems

by

Luong Thanh Tran / Katarina Dulkova

SOCIETAS 2013

Bibliographic information published by the Deutsche Nationalbibliothek

The Deutsche Nationalbibliothek lists this publication in the Deutsche Nationalbibliografie; detailed bibliographic data are available in the Internet at http://dnb.dnb.de.

Bibliographische Information der Deutschen Nationalbibliothek

Die Deutsche Nationalbibliothek verzeichnet diese Publikation in der deutschen Nationalbibliographie; detaillierte bibliographische Daten sind im Internet über <http://dnb.ddb.de> abrufbar.

Societas Verlagsgesellschaft KG, Jena, 2013
Alle Rechte vorbehalten / All rights reserved

ISBN 978-3-944420-07-3

www.societas-verlag.de
www.societas-publishers.com

# Inhaltsverzeichnis

*Luong Thanh Tran*
Relocation of Polluted Industries
Trade Liberalization in Developing Countries and Environmental Issues . . . . . . . . . . . . . . . . . . . . . . . . . . . .   7

*Katarina Dulkova*
The Political Economy of Agriculture Protection in the Western World . . . . . . . . . . . . . . . . . . . . . . . . . . . . . . .  27

# Relocation of Polluted Industries Trade Liberalization in Developing Countries and Environmental Issues

Luong Thanh Tran

| | | |
|---|---|---|
| I. | Introduction | 8 |
| II. | The relation between trade and environmental issues | 9 |
| | 1. The Pollution Haven Hypothesis | 10 |
| | 2. How trade affects the environment: Scale, composition and technique effects | 11 |
| | 3. Income and the Environment: Environmental Kuznets Curve | 14 |
| III. | Environmental policy | 16 |
| | 1. Race to the Bottom? | 16 |
| | 2. International spillover effects | 18 |
| | 3. International policy | 19 |
| IV. | Conclusion | 21 |
| Reference | | 22 |

# I. Introduction

Trade liberalization has been no doubt benefiting developing countries in term of economic growth. China and India are great examples of trade liberalization's success. Wacziarg and Welch (2008) claimed that in the period 1950-1998, countries which liberalized their trade regimes obtained an average annual growth rates about 1.5% higher than before liberalization. However, prospect may come along with a greater cost in long term development. It is observed that through the process of trade liberalization, with laxer environmental regulations and having comparative advantage in producing pollution intensive goods, developing countries are potentially becoming havens for dirty products.

This paper will examine the relation between trade liberalization and environmental issues, especially in developing countries, through a number of theories and hypotheses. There has been long debate about the validity of the "Pollution Haven Hypothesis", together with mixed arguments about scale, composition, technique effects of trade toward environmental problems. From another perspective, the answer for the question whether trade benefits or degrades the environment may lie in the Environmental Kuznets Curve, as it models the link between income and pollution levels.

Furthermore, environmental policy will be analyzed as a controversy for the "Race to the Bottom" theory, which states that governments try to lower environmental standards to gain comparative advantage in international competitiveness. The theory may be supported by "Stuck at the Bottom" theory by Porter (1999) about developing countries' inability in getting out of the problems. However, it may be countered by the "Race to Top" theory by Vogel (2000), states the reverse in case of protectionism. In the next part, a theoretical approach of the international spillover effects from Sinn (2003) will be explained in the case of pollution and the need for international coordination.

Finally, from developing countries' perspectives, international policy and relocation of pollution will also be discussed, especially with Peters and Hertwich (2008)'s analysis of shifting the measurement of pollution from production-based inventories to consumption-based inventories.

## II. The relation between trade and environmental issues

Tobey (1990) defined a polluted industry as one where pollution abatement costs in the United States were 1.85% or more of total costs e.g. pulp and paper, mining, iron and steel, primary non-ferrous metals and chemicals. He created an ordinal variable ranging from one to seven to measure the level of stringency of a country's environmental policies for international comparisons. World Bank researchers Low and Yeats (1992) also had similar list of pollution intensive industries, selected on the basis of pollution abatement cost in the United States.

From theoretical approaches of Hechkscher Ohlin, Rybzinski, Krugman models, it is commonly known that trade is inevitable for a country to achieve higher growth rates. Nowadays, economic growth becomes one of the most important key objectives for most of the developing countries. These countries are liberalizing to promote trade and FDI for the development of the nation. However, according to Fredriksson (1999), reduced trade barriers lead to specialization in pollution intensive industries in developing countries. While developed countries are having stricter environmental regulations, through the process of liberalization, developing countries are less concerned about the environmental issues.

The relation between trade and environmental issues has been much of a controversy. Ulph (1997) argued that more trade results in increased consumption and production, hence causes more environmental degradation. Therefore, damage caused to the environment out weights benefits from trade liberalization. Anderson and Strutt (1996) expressed concern about deforestation and chemical use as the effect of increased world commodity prices on developing countries production.

However, some other economists such as Copeland and Taylor (2004) claimed that economic growth has positive impacts on the environment. By analyzing the income effect in the Environmental Kuznets Curve, they conclude that there is strong evidence that income effect raises the environmental quality.

## 1. The Pollution Haven Hypothesis

One of the dominated discussions about the effects of trade among countries on the environment is the Pollution Haven Hypothesis. According to Copeland and Taylor (2004), there should be distinguish between Pollution Haven Effect and Pollution Haven Hypothesis.

Basically, Pollution Haven Effect is the effect when developed countries tighten environmental policy, which leads to the decline of productions hence reduction of net exports of pollution goods from developed countries. Moreover, capitals from polluted industries would flow from developed countries to developing countries, where the regulations on environmental issues are laxer. This may also result in plants and factories reallocation. Pollution Haven Effect simply shows that environmental regulations have effects on changing in trade volumes.

Pollution Haven Effect is only one of the determinants for the changing in trade volumes. When Pollution Haven Effect is strong enough to be the key factor for the direction of trade and investment flows, Copeland and Taylor (2004) considered it become Pollution Haven Hypothesis. Especially when developing countries liberalize their trade barriers, with weaker environmental policy they will have a comparative advantage in producing pollution intensive goods, and also attract foreign investment in these sectors. On the other hand, the cost of production in developing countries are lower than in developed countries, due to relatively lower wage rates, which would speed up the process of migrating polluted industries from developed to developing countries. Liddle (2001) showed that the simple impact of the Pollution Haven Hypothesis happens when low environmental standards become the driving force of comparative advantages, which results in the shift in trade pattern.

The consequences of the Pollution Haven Hypothesis might be severe: trade liberalization would increase total world pollution and the citizens in the areas with polluted industries are likely to be harmed most, hence developing countries would suffer from lower welfare and other negative effects from pollution. The process that rich countries seek pollution havens in poorer countries may lead to an international spillover of changing in environmental regulations, which will be discussed later as a "Race to the Bottom" problem of environmental policy. Moreover, if developed countries deal with the environmental problems by continuing shifting polluted industries to developing countries, then the world would run out of places to shift those productions to, hence poor countries may not be able to get out of the problems, especially in the long term till the point that the abatement costs are too huge to remove already set factories and infrastructures. Porter (1999) proposed the "Stuck at the Bottom" as the consequence of Race to the Bottom hypothesis for the unresponsiveness from political institutions toward the environmental issues.

Empirical works from Low and Yeats (1992) proved that Pollution Haven Hypothesis is indeed making developing countries shift to pollution intensive goods. They found that in the period of 1965-1988, developed countries reduce exports of dirty goods from 20% to 16%, while developing countries gain comparative advantage in those industries, with Eastern Europe's exports of dirty goods increase from 21% to 28%, and Latin America's increase from 17% to 21%. In addition, using data for the period 1965-1995, Mani and Wheeler (1997) found that the net exports of dirty goods in developing countries coincide with abatement costs in the OECD countries, hinder the capital flows of polluted industries from developed to developing countries.

## 2. How trade affects the environment: Scale, composition and technique effects

According to Grossman and Krueger (1991) and several other authors, trade affects the environment through three main ways. Scale effect changes the overall level of economic activity, composition effect changes the type of economic activity through specialization, and technique effect can lead to change in the environmental intensity of production.

The *scale effect* implies that trade is positively related to the pollution. Total amount of pollution increases along with the expansion of economic activities, which are mainly results of increases in trade. For example, a 1% increase in economy scale would result in 1% increase in pollution level. In other aspect, more trade among countries and continents leads to more use of transportation, hence increasing the amount of air pollution from flights and ships. Peters (2008) criticized the territorial system boundary used by the United National Framework Convention on Climate Change (UNFCCC) for excluding international transportation and potentially causing carbon leakage.

The *composition effect* relates the comparative advantage to trade practices. Due to Heckscher Ohlin model, each trading country specializes in the sector in which it gains comparative advantage. In a static model of two countries produce a continuum of goods, each differing in pollution intensity, Copeland and Taylor (1994) showed that the higher income countries always choose stronger environmental protection, and specialize in relative clean goods. It is observed that developed countries enforce strict regulations and are less competitive in producing pollution intensive products, while developing countries have laxer environmental regulations. In this way developing countries have more chances to specialize in pollution intensive industries. Reducing trade barriers reinforce the tendency for developing countries to specialize and export dirty goods.

By examining macroeconomic indicators including industry-level economic and environmental data for Vietnam, Mani and Jha (2006) concluded from their analysis that there has been a change in output composition in Vietnam industries that parallels the trade liberalization of the economy:

From 2000 to 2003, Vietnam's domestic productions have become more specialized in the production from dirty industries to clean industries, especially manufacturing output from water pollution intensive sectors (composition effect on domestic production). As a result of the United States-Vietnam Bilateral Trade Agreement – USBTA trade treaty in 2001, the United States has becoming the largest market for Vietnamese exports. Along with rocket rising of 128 percent increasing exports to the US, which accounts for 82 percent of total export growth in 2002, Vietnam has become more specialized in share of exports from dirty industries relative to clean industries (composition effect on trade flows). From 1997 to 2000, Vietnam has become more specialized in the exports from dirty industries relative to clean industries (the composition effect on exports). Sectors that have highest growth in exports are textile (91 percent), leather (49 percent), and rubber products (26 percent). Of these the textile industry is large consumer for industrial chemicals, hence increased textiles exports would go along with increases of industrial chemicals. Similarly, export revenues from craft villages have increased significantly in recent years, which are major sources of toxic and water pollution. There has been also greater inflow of foreign investment into toxic pollution intensive sectors. This result has statistically proven the existence of composition effects on domestic production, trade flows and exports in the case of Vietnam.

However, Cole and Elliott (2003) argued that pollution-intensive sectors may be subject to opposing forces of comparative advantage since these sectors are also typically capital intensive. Moreover, regions with low environmental regulations tend to be those that are the least capital abundant. They examine whether compositional changes in pollution arising from trade liberalization originate due to differences in capital-labor endowments and/or differences in environmental regulations. Their result is trade liberalization reduces the pollution intensity of output.

It is argued that *technique effect* further shows the pollution per unit product may decrease with the increasing trade. By increasing trade and FDI, modern technology transfers from developed countries to the developing countries. These modern technologies are assumed to be more efficient and cleaner than the traditional production methods; therefore developing countries can produce same products with less pollution. Multinational firms may follow the same technology in their home countries, generally apply stricter environmental regulations even in other countries, and it may be accessible for them to use the same technology in all locations. In addition, increasing trade leads to increases in competition, which may force firms to adopt more efficient and environment protection technologies in order to match international quality standard.

Late industrializing countries have the opportunity to learn from experiences and to leapfrog to less costly and more efficient environmental technologies. Improvements in technologies provide newer and less polluting production processes, which can go along with high industrial growth rates and rapid turnover. In Sonnenfeld (1998)'s study of the pulp industry of Thailand, he concluded that the country's late industrialization profited from the incorporation of advanced environmental technology. By examining the Ecological Modernization Theory with a case study of Vietnam, Jos et al. (2000) claimed that developments in Vietnam such as economic liberalization, privatization and internationalization and the slowly starting democratization of governance offer ecological modernization-inspired opportunities to incorporate environmental considerations in the economic development of the country.

Moreover, increasing trade results in growth in income of developing countries, hence create interest in cleaner environment. This will be discussed further later in the context by analyzing the Environmental

Kuznets Curve. Therefore, due to technique effect, increasing trade leads to increases in environmental quality.

In general, by isolating the scale, composition and technique effect, Copeland and Taylor (1994) showed that free trade increase world pollution, while similar growth in the developing countries lowers pollution. However, unilateral transfers from developed countries to developing country reduce worldwide pollution.

## 3. Income and the Environment: Environmental Kuznets Curve

One of the most important factors to differentiate rich and poor countries is income level. The Environmental Kuznets curve is a concept of an inverted U-shape relation between pollution level and income per capita. As countries get richer, assumed mostly from the effects of international trade, pollution level rises at early stages but falls later. In another aspect, increased incomes may lead to increased pollution in developing countries and lower pollution in developed countries.

**Figure 1:**
Environmental Kuznets curve for sulfur emissions. Source: Panayotou (1993) and Stern, Common & Barbier (1996).

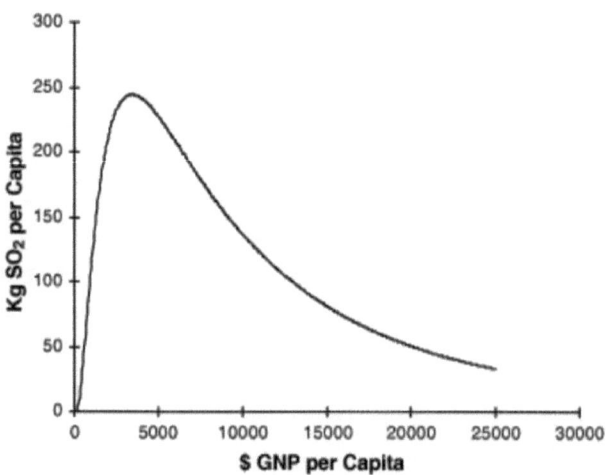

Due to the scale effect, if there were no change in technology, input-output ratio or the structure of the economy, pollution level would increase in line with growing aggregate output of the economy. However, Adreoni and Levinson (2001) showed that there could be economies or diseconomies of scale of pollution, depending on variants of polluted industries.

Increasing trade and growth of the economy eventually leads to structural change of the economy. In earlier phases of development, developing countries shift from agriculture to heavy industrial sector, which increases emissions. After reaching a certain point of income, the economy would shift toward service sector, hence supposedly lower the pollution level.

Moreover, by conducting studies in Sweden, Hökby and Söderqvist (2002) found that income elasticity of willingness to pay for improvements in environmental quality is positive, which implies that environmental quality is a normal good. If this holds true, increased incomes resulting from trade liberalization will generate increased demand for improvement of the environment. Nordstrom and Vaughan (1999) argued that the higher the income per capita, the more people care about cleaner environment, hence further explaining the downward part of the Environmental Kuznets Curve.

Furthermore, by quantifying the effect using pooled cross-country and time-series data, Suri and Chapman (1998) proposed that imports and exports are considered to have the most influence impact on the shape of the Environmental Kuznets Curve. Exports of manufactured goods by developing countries is an important factor in generating the upward sloping portion of the Environmental Kuznets Curve and imports by developed countries have contributed to the downward slope. By summarizing previous works by other economists and running econometric tests on sulfur emissions, Stern (2004) showed that using concentration data, all turning point estimates are less than $ 6.000, with the exception of Kaufmann et al. (1998).

In his previous studies, Stern et al. (1996) suggested that economic growth does not harm the global sustainability, and there are no environmental limits to growth. He claims that the empirical results of the Environmental Kuznets Curve have been mixed. Studies from Mani and Wheeler (1999) showed the industrial water pollution rises sharply with increasing income but remains constant after a certain level. Rothman (1998) showed that the Environmental Kuznets Curve does not hold in the case of consumption based pollution like $CO_2$ and municipal waste. In another study, by using large and globally samples to analyze the Environmental Kuznets curve for Sulfur, Stern and Common (2001) found that reduction in emissions are time-related rather than income-related.

## III. Environmental policy

There has been much discussion on the linkage between trade policies of both developed and developing countries and the environmental concerns, which has been the subject of debate between the trade policy community and environmentalists. According to Mani and Jha (2006), free traders fear that environmental protection may be used as an excuse in order to gain domestic protection for some economic sectors, while environmentalists have concerns that free trade may be used as an excuse for ecological dumping with higher economic growth goals. Moreover, the question on how to reduce the global pollution level requires not only regulations from domestic perspective but also international coordination among countries.

### 1. Race to the Bottom?

According to Nader et al. (1993), Race to the Bottom hypothesis refers to the situation when without international coordination, governments sacrifice environmental quality and the welfare of their citizens to become globally competitive.

Rauscher (1994) claimed that by putting environmental issues underregulated, this can create a process of ecological dumping, in which governments use lax environmental standards in order to protect domestic firms in international competition and achieve trade-related economic policy goals. Suppose that environmental standards in a country are lower than the other countries, domestic producers in that country benefit from lower costs than their foreign competitors. As a sequence, other countries start to lower their respective environmental standards in order to support their industries, hence create a harmonization of environmental policy, all countries use the same but low environ mental standards. Konisky (2007) claimed that the Race to the Bottom argument is an example of the Prisoner's Dilemma game, when the equilibrium outcome is suboptimal, since states would be better off maintaining their low environmental standards.

Studies from Ederington and Minier (2003) support the Race to the Bottom hypothesis when they find evidence of the use of environmental regulations as the secondary means to protect domestic industries. Waltz and Wellisch (1997) showed that governments of exporting countries choose free trade over environmental issues, even if countries subsidize their local industries indirectly via ecological dumping. Porter (1999) claimed that Race to the Bottom is likely to be in rapidly industrialized countries, and competitiveness concerns exert downward pressure on environmental standards, creating a "Stuck at the Bottom" problem, with the unresponsiveness from political institutions.

However, by looking at actual government behavior, Wheeler (2001) found that increases in trade go along with evidence of improvements in air quality and other environmental indicators, thus reject the hypothesis. Copeland and Taylor (1994) argued that lowering environmental standards is an inefficient policy to subsidize domestic industries. The reason is environmental control costs are relatively small, according to Dean (1992), hence lowering environmental standards creates costs on others and encourages lobbies activities from firms. In contrast, it is more likely that some developed countries employ stricter environmental policy in order to protect their own industries. Mani and Jha (2006) argued that environmental tariffs may be used against trading partners which have inadequate environmental standards as a disguised kind of protection for domestic firms. Vogel (2000) proposed the reverse "Race to the Top" hypothesis, by implying that economic openness and capital mobility encourage countries level up environmental standards. When domestic producers and environmentalists form alliances, if both groups are politically influential and domestic firms are more efficient at incorporating environmental standards than foreign firms, the government might raise environmental standards in order to protect domestic industries. He gives an example of the strict German automobile emission controls in the 1980's, which protected the domestic market when Italian and French car firms found the controls too costly to follow.

According to Copeland and Taylor (2004), the major affects from the Race to the Bottom issues create to developing countries are increasing in political support for demands for connecting environmental standards with trade agreements and policy harmonization. Suranovic (2002) showed that there is increasing support for including labor and environmental agreements in the World Trade Organization, which might require minimum environmental and labor protection (as counter to social dumping) across countries and allow countries to use import restrictions to punish violations. According to Ulph (1997), if a country is affected by pollution from other country, trade policy may be used by the affected country to reduce the damage when they trade with the offending country.

## 2. International spillover effects

There seems to be no better example for the international spillover effects than pollution. Air pollution, water pollution... will not stay within borders of different countries. In fact, pollution in one country affects the utility and welfare of citizens in the others. Ulph (1997) showed that production and consumption activities in one country may lead to global environmental effects in the form of trans-boundary pollution such as acid rain, or other spillover effects such as depletion of the ozone layer. A single country can enrich itself at the expense of other countries by neglecting the environment, but if all countries neglect the environment problems, they will eventually end up damaging themselves.

From the theoretical approaches of Sinn (2003), the opening of trade and systems competition would lead to ecological dumping from environmental policy perspectives, if there were no such benevolent "supranational planner" to correct the market failures, nor any kind of international coordination. It is assumed that every country must bear the costs from the international spillovers of pollution. Unregulated firms create negative externalities toward the environments, but by implying an ecological (or Pigovian) tax per unit of emission, the governments can step by step lowering emission level in the long term.

In the model of international spillovers, Sinn (2003) argued that every country plays Cournot i.e. each country optimizes its waste emissions under the assumption that its behavior has no influence on the emissions of the other countries. However, each country just takes the pollution on its own inhabitants into account and neglects the effect on the other countries, there for the tax rate will be too low.

**Figure 2:**
The optimal Pigovian tax rate with international spillovers. Source: Sinn H-W. (2003)

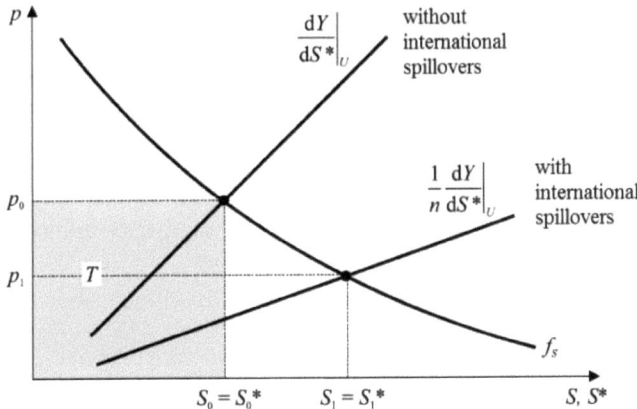

The (benevolent) government acts as to maximize the citizen's utility by setting the amount of emissions S and therewith indirectly the Pigovian tax rate p on firms. T is tax revenue transferred to households. In the case of international spillover, the Pareto optimal pollution policy is given by the equality between the national marginal product of the waste emission and the sum of the world marginal damage that this emission causes. The more countries, the larger the externality $S_1 > S_0$, but the lower the tax rate $p_1 < p_0$, and the country will engage in ecological dumping. This is a strong argument in favor of a coordinated environmental policy across countries. However, all countries have incentives to deviate, therefore only collective action can overcome the suboptimal allocation problem.

## 3. International policy

Since environmental issues have the nature of international spillover effects, some countries may take the benefits from the free riding behavior. The problem could be treated with international policy coordination among nations. Freytag and Wangler (2008) showed that due to its nature, climate change protection can be considered as a public good, hence it requires the contribution from all the countries in order to solve the Prisoner's Dilemma and reach collective action goals. They give an example of the Kyoto Protocol: under the assumption that all the other countries ratify the protocol, if a country does not ratify the contract, in the short run it would realize its winning margin at the level of international competitiveness.

However, Copeland and Taylor (2004) argued that policy in most developed countries is commonly set via a political process and not necessarily in a way that promotes social efficiency. Therefore, an attempt to enforce such harmonization at global level would lead to much inefficiency and may be unworkable. They point out that there is more potential for such an approach to work better in regional trade agreements (such as the EU), where countries have similarity in income and their capacity to deal with environmental issues.

Although most developing countries tend to oppose global harmonization, high environmental standards from developed countries may benefit developing countries. Wilson and Tsunehiro (2003) found that in some cases the largest gainers of harmonization would be developing countries. In their studies, if the international food safety standards are applied, the world food exports (mostly from developing countries) would rise by $ 38.8 billion, hence create larger increases in world trade for food products. Limão (2002) claimed that trade and environmental policies are strategic complements, linking between trade agreements and environmental agreements may result in greater cooperation in both issues, including reductions in tariffs and improvement in environmental standards, hence raise overall world welfare.

The most well-known international coordination to date may be the Kyoto Protocol signed in 1997 under the UNFCC with the goals of reducing global emissions of greenhouse gases (GHG). In which, developing countries have the better benefits of no binding targets, while annex I & II countries (dominantly developed countries in Europe plus Australia) must have binding target. It is argued that this may further support the Pollution Havens Hypothesis of changing composition of production toward more polluted industries in lower income states.

However, Peter and Hertwich (2008) argued that the measurement of pollution emitted should be shifted from production-based to consumption-based, which means that emission bounded in goods produced in developing countries should be counted for developed countries' consumption, since consumption-based GHG inventories have many advantages over production-based GHG inventories. This changing in measurement can be effective in the long term, reduce the importance of pollution commitments for developing countries and encourage the green technology in those countries, which supports the Ecological Modernization Theory. Furthermore, he also claims that constructing GHG inventories using a country's economic activity instead of geographic territory will solve allocation issues for international activities such as international transportation and carbon capture and storage. However, in another study later the same year, Peters (2008) also argued that it may be more difficult to implement consumption-based inventories directly to the climate policy, due to increased uncertainty and a wide system boundary. From developing countries' perspectives, it is both efficient and fair for developed countries to bear a larger share of costs toward environmental issues. In another aspect, Costanza et al. (1997) proposed to shift the taxation of income and labor to ecological damage and consumption of natural resources. All of these changing measurements may have positive effects in the long term development and counter the negative effects of spreading environmental problems.

## IV. Conclusion

Generally, through the paper we can conclude that trade liberalization in developing countries has negative correlations with improvement in environmental quality. Through changes in scale, composition and technique effects, some developing countries in one hand have comparative advantages in producing polluted intensive products, but in other hand benefit from adapting cleaner technologies as late industrialized states. Race to the Bottom theory has been proven to have little empirical evidence to support, but international coordination must be met in order to solve the problem of pollution spillover effects. The process of limiting polluted industries could be improved in many ways, two of these are shifting the measurement of pollution from production-based inventories to consumption-based inventories, and shifting the taxation on "goods" to "bads" in term of ecological damage and consumption of natural resources. The question is how to effectively implement these policies and form better international coordinations among countries in order to reduce the world's pollution level in one hand, but also achieve other economic objects such as promoting international trade and growth in the other hand, especially in the case of developing countries.

# Reference

*Anderson, K. & Strutt, A.* (1996), "On measuring the environment impact of agricultural trade liberalisation", in M.E. Bredahl, N. Ballinger, J.C. Dunmore, and T.L. Roe (eds), *Agriculture, Trade, and the Environment: Discovering and Measuring the Critical Linkages* (Boulder, CO: Westview Press, 1996, pp. 151-172).

*Andreoni, J. & A. Levinson* (2001), "The simple analytics of the environmental Kuznets curve" *Journal of Public Economics*, 80 (2001), pp. 269-286.

*Cole, Matthew A. and Robert J.R. Elliott* (2003), "Determining the trade-environment composition effect: the role of capital, labor and environmental regulations", *Journal of Environmental Economics and Management*, Volume 46, Issue 3, November 2003, Pages 363-383.

*Costanza R., J. Cumberland, H. Daly, R. Goodland, R. Norgaard* (1997), *Introduction to Ecological Economics*, St. Lucie Press, USA.

*Copeland, Brian R. and M. Scott Taylor* (1994), "North-South Trade and the Environment", *Quarterly Journal of Economics*, Volume 109, Issue 3, August 1994, 755-787.

*Copeland, Brian R. and M. Scott Taylor* (2004), "Trade, Growth, and the Environment" *Journal of Economic Literature*, Volume XLII (March 2004), pp. 7-71.

*Dean, Judith M.* (1992), "Trade and the Environment: A survey of the literatire", in Patrick Low, ed., *International Trade and the Evironment: World Bank Discussion Papers* (Washington, DC: World Bank, 1992).

*Ederington, W.J. and J. Minier* (2003), "Is environmental policy a secondary trade barrier? An empirical analysis,", *Canadian Journal of Economics* 36: 137-154.

*Fredriksson, P.G.* (1999) "The Political Economy of Trade Liberalization and Environmental Policy", *Southern Economic Journal*, 65(3), 1999, pp. 513-525.

*Freytag, Andreas and L. Wangler* (2008) "Strategic Trade Policy as Response to Climate Change?", *Jena Economic Research Paper*, No. 2008-001.

*Grossman, Gene M. and Alan B. Krueger* (1991), "Environmental Impacts of a North American Free Trade Agreement", *NBER Working Paper*, No. 3914, November 1991.

*Hökby, Stina & Tore Söderqvist* (2003) "Elasticities of Demand and Willingness to Pay for Environmental Services in Sweden", *Environmental and Resource Economics*, November 2003, Volume 26, Issue 3, pp 361-383.

*Jos Frijns, Phung Thuy Phuong & Arthur P.J. Mol* (2000), Ecological Modernisation Theory and Industrialising Economies: The Case of Viet Nam, *Developing countries, Environmental Politics*, 9:1, 257-292.

*Kaufmann R.K., B. Davidsdottir, S. Garnham, P. Pauly*, "The determinants of atmospheric $SO_2$ concentrations: Reconsidering the environmental Kuznets curve", *Ecological Economy*, 25 (1998), pp. 209-220.

*Konisky, David M.* (2007), "Regulatory Competition and Environmental Enforcement: Is There a Race to the Bottom?", *American Journal of Political Science*, Volume 51, Issue 4, Pages 853-872, October 2007.

*Liddle, Brantley* (2001), "Free trade and the environment-development system", *Ecological Economics*, Volume 39, Issue 1, October 2001, Pages 21-36.

*Limão, N.* (2002), "Trade Policy, Cross-border Externalities and Lobbies: Do Linked Agreements Enforce More Cooperative Outcomes?", *UMD Center for International Economics WP 02-01*, University of Maryland at College Park.

*Low, P. and A. Yeates* (1992), "Do 'dirty' Industries Migrate", in Low P (ed), *International Trade and the Environment, World Bank discussion paper*, No. 159, 89-104.

*Mani, M. and D. Wheeler* (1999), "In Search of Pollution Havens?", *Trade, global policy, and the environment*, Parts 63-402.

*Mani, M. and D. Wheeler* (1997), "In search of pollution havens?: dirty industry migration in the world economy", *World Bank Working Paper*, No. 16.

*Mani, Muthukumara and Shreyasi Jha* (2006), "Trade Liberalization and the Environment in Vietnam", *World Bank Policy Research Working Paper* 3879, April 2006.

*Nader, Ralph, William Greider, Margaret Atwood, David Philips, Pat Choate* (1993), *"The Case Against Free Trade: Gatt, Nafta and the Globalization of Corporate Power"*, Earth Island Press.

*Nordström H., S. Vaughan* (1999), "Special Studies 4: Trade and Environment", *World Trade Organization*, Geneva.

*Panayotou, T.* (1993), "Empirical tests and policy analysis of environmental degradation at different stages of economic development", *Working Paper WP238, Technology and Employment Programme*, International Labour Office, Geneva.

*Peters P. Glen, and Edgar G. Hertwich* (2008), "Post-Kyoto greenhouse gas inventories: production versus consumption", *Climatic Change,* Volume 86, Issue 1-2, pp 51-66.

*Peters P. Glen* (2008), "From production-based to consumption-based national emission inventories", *Ecological Economics,* Volume 65, Issue 1, 15, March 2008, Pages 13-23.

*Porter, Gareth* (1999), "Trade Competition and Pollution Standards: "Race to the Bottom" or "Stuck at the Bottom", *The Journal of Environment Development,* June 1999, Volume 8, No. 2, pp 133-151.

*Rauscher, M.* (1994), "On ecological dumping" *Oxford Economic Papers* – New Series Volume 46, Supplement: S. Pages 822-840, Published: October 1994.

*Rothman, S. Dale* (1998), "Environmental Kuznets curves – Real progress or passing the buck?: A case for consumption-based approaches" – *Ecological Economics,* Volume 25, Issue 2, May 1998, Pages 177-194.

*Sinn, Hans-Werner* (2003), *"The New Systems Competition"*, *Yrjö Jahnsson Lectures*, Basil Blaclwell, Oxford, Chap 5.

*Sonnenfeld, David A.* (1998), "From Brown to Green? Late Industrialization, Social Conflict, and Adoption of Environmental Technologies in Thailand's Pulp Industry", *Organization Environment,* March 1998, Volume 11, No. 1, 59-87.

*Stern D.I., M.S. Common, E.B. Barbier* (1996), "Economic growth and environmental degradation: The environmental Kuznets curve and sustainable development", *World Development,* 24 (1996), pp. 1151-1160.

*Stern I. David, Michael S. Common* (2001), "Is There an Environmental Kuznets Curve for Sulfur?" *Journal of Environmental Economics and Management*, Volume 41, Issue 2, March 2001, Pages 162-178.

*Stern, I. David* (2004), "The Rise and Fall of the Environmental Kuznets Curve" *World Development*, Volume 32, Issue 8, August 2004, Pages 1419-1439.

*Suranovic S.* (2002), "International Labour and Environmental Standards Agreements: Is This Fair Trade?", *The World Economy*, 25(2): 231-245.

*Suri, Vivek and Duane Chapman* (1998), "Economic growth, trade and energy: implications for the environmental Kuznets curve", *Ecological Economics*, Volume 25, Issue 2, May 1998, Pages 195-208.

*Tobey, J. A.* (1990), "The Effects of Domestic Environmental Policies on Patterns of World Trade: An Empirical Test.", *Kyklos, International Review for Social Sciences* 43, 191-209, doi: 10.1111/j.1467-6435.1990.tb00207.x.

*Ulph, A.* (1997), "International trade and the environment: a survey of recent economic analysis", in H. Folmer and T. Tietenberg, *International Handbook of Environmental and Resource Economics*, (Cheltenham: Edward Elgar, 1997, pp. 205-242).

*Vogel D.* (2000), "Environmental Regulation and Economic Integration," *Journal of International Economic Law*: 265-279.

*Wacziarg, Romain and Karen Horn Welch* (2008), "Trade Liberalization and Growth: New Evidence", *World Bank Economic Review*, Volume 22, Issue 2, pp. 187-231, 2008.

*Walz, Uwe and Dietmar Wellisch* (1997), "Is free trade in the interest of exporting countries when there is ecological dumping?", *Journal of Public Economics*, Volume 66, Issue 2, 1. November 1997, Pages 275-291.

*Wheeler D.* (January 2001), "Racing to the Bottom? Foreign Investment and Air Pollution inDeveloping Countries", *Policy Research Working Paper*: 2524.

*Wilson, John S., Otsuki, Tsunehiro* (2003), "Food Safety and Trade: Winners and Losers in a Non-harmonized World,", *Journal-of-Economic-Integration*, 18(2): 266-87.

# The Political Economy of Agriculture Protection in the Western World

KATARINA DULKOVA

| | | |
|---|---|---|
| I. | Introduction | 28 |
| II. | The Paradox of Agriculture | 29 |
| III. | Theoretical explanations for Agricultural Protectionism | 31 |
| | 1. The Political Economy of Protectionism | 31 |
| | 2. The Political Economy of Agricultural Protectionism | 34 |
| IV. | Agricultural Protectionism in Western World | 39 |
| | 1. The EU and Agricultural Protectionism | 39 |
| | 2. The WTO Doha Round of Trade Negotiations | 41 |
| V. | Conclusion | 43 |
| Reference | | 45 |

# I. Introduction

The issue of liberalization of world agricultural trade is one of the key matters of recent economic discourses. With the conclusion of the Uruguay Round Agreement on Agriculture (URAA) in 1994, principles applied successfully by GATT for past half of a century to trade in manufactured products, were finally made applicable to trade in agricultural products. This was a surprise to many, as agricultural protection has been and still is a subject to powerful agricultural producers lobby.

Moreover, agriculture remains a very sensitive topic for almost every member states of WTO and is still considered as a sector which needs special attention. This is principally due to the fact that protectionism in agriculture is eminently higher than in other sectors of economy. Therefore, negotiations on agricultural liberalization in the subsequent Doha Round of the WTO deserve rightly top priority. The aim of the negotiations is successful continuation of the reform process in the agricultural trade and achievement of goals set forth by the member states; this includes substantial cuts in domestic subsidies and tariffs, and fair market access for all countries.

While these efficiency objectives come from standard economic analyses, one has to take into account not only the economic factors, but also the historical, ideological and mainly political factors that shape the current trade policies and the policy-making process. In order to get complete picture of reasons for persistence of agricultural protectionism, an explanation of political economy of trade theories is necessary. To make the interpretation of trade theory comprehensible, one has to turn to public choice approaches and models dealing principally with the specific interest groups.

The basic purpose of this paper is to present a brief overview of the main political economy theories and their application to the agricultural trade policies. In doing so, it will shortly review the main findings from the political economy literature and highlight the differences in agricultural policies used by the developing and developed countries. Moreover, it will demonstrate the necessity to take a look at both economical and political factors, when explaining the persistence of agricultural protectionism, and also shortly mention the consumer based approach to agriculture protection. The paper will further briefly discuss some protectionist measures used by the European Union, demonstrate the connection between the reforms in the WTO and Common Agricultural

Policy of EU, and will conclude with some observations about the last WTO Round of negotiations, regarding the agricultural trade.

## II. The Paradox of Agriculture

When observing the national agricultural policies throughout the world, one comes across an interesting "income effect": the governments in richer countries, where the agriculture represents only a small share of economy, tend to subsidize agriculture or provide price-support measures for farmers, at the expense of their food consumers, while governments in poorer countries tend to tax their agriculture, despite the large share of farmer population. In other words, developed countries protect their agricultural sector while less developed countries discriminate against their agriculture. This maybe illogical pattern is known as the "development paradox": agricultural policies in both developed and developing countries seem to support relatively wealthy minority and exploit relatively poor majority. The subsidized farmers (minority) in richer countries have often incomes higher than the average, while taxed farmers in poorer countries (majority) have incomes lower than the average.[1] There were several studies published in order to explain why, as countries get richer and the amount of their farmers shrinks, unfairness towards agriculture diminishes and possibly turns into positive support. One clarification lies in the limited revenues and taxation options of the less-developed countries with large agricultural sectors, and the small ability of them to protect their agriculture.[2]

According to the Bilal (2000), there was a study undertaken by the World Bank Project on the Political Economy of Agricultural Pricing Policy, examining agricultural pricing policies in 18 developing countries, with the founding that the impact of indirect policies (foreign exchange rate policies and the general trade regime) is greater than the impact of direct interventions, considering their effect on producer prices and purchasing power of the prices for farmers. Yet, farmers' lobbying efforts are focused on direct measures (affecting the agrarian prices), rather than lobbying to change the macroeconomic policy, which might be of course much more difficult. Such lobbying could be against other interest groups 'stakes, such as manufacturing producers group. Generally, countries using a lot of state intervention in the

---

[1] *Timmer* (1991).
[2] *Weiberg* and *Bekker* (2011).

economy show significant discrimination in their agricultural sector too. However, this intervention is usually positive for industry and negative for agriculture. Countries favor their industrial sectors at the expense of agriculture, reason being the general belief that support to industry will boost the growth and development of a country.

Another important founding of the before mentioned study was the identification of common characteristics of governmental interventions in agriculture:

> "1. Agricultural inputs are almost always subsidized.
> 2. Import-competing agricultural products are protected or subsidized.
> 3. Exportable agricultural commodities are generally discriminated against (taxed)."[3]

Considering the "development paradox" in richer countries, the common analysis states that persistence of agricultural protection is only hard to clarify economically, as it's of common knowledge that in the western world the costs of protecting agricultural sector outweigh the benefits to their societies as whole.[4] Agricultural protectionism in developed countries is irrational because subsidies are granted usually to financially inefficient producers, causing overproduction, negatively affecting international food prices, hurting exporters from developing countries and even damaging the environment. The reason, why the governments don't eliminate those subsidies, is the high power of interest groups and their influence over political actors. However, there might be more arguments for agricultural protectionism than that.

Some studies claim that the maintenance of protectionist agricultural policies in developed countries may occur because of country's strategic interests in fostering the agribusiness sector. These interests of state agents include safeguarding state's self-sufficiency in agricultural production, as this might prevent potential instability in international food production and distribution. In times of crisis, it may be disadvantageous to be dependent on foreign food suppliers. Second reason for aid to agricultural sector could be the support of industrial,

---

[3] Saunossi Bilal in *Negotiating the Future of Agricultural Policies: Agricultural Trade and the "Millennium" WTO Round*, edited by Sanoussi Bilal and Pavlos Pezaros, Kluwer Law International, 2000. Chapter 3: The Political Economy of Agricultural Policies and Negotiations p. 81.

[4] *Thies, Porche* (2007).

technological or commercial enterprises, which are dependent on agricultural outcomes, primarily to secure the production in other sectors. These arguments are important for any country which takes part in competitive international system.[5]

Nevertheless, these statements don't explain the fact that, contrary to common logic, a small minority of farmers (which makes a share less than 5% of the labor force in majority of developed countries[6]) have succeed in obtaining such a high level of governmental support, whereas in developing countries, where the population of farmers represents the majority of workers, are being exploited. To find a proper answer to this question, one has to take a deeper look in the literature of the political economy of agriculture.

# III. Theoretical explanations for Agricultural Protectionism

This chapter will start with a controversial question: Why is there so much support for farmers in developed countries? Moreover why is agriculture protected at such different levels by otherwise similarly developed countries? Several explanations could be founded in the literature of the political economy of agriculture. To begin with the interpretation for this "anomaly", one has to consider a wide range of hypotheses about government's decision-making from the political economy literature. Many of these hypotheses were formulated rather in a general way or applied to different industries in specific countries. This chapter will concentrate on examination and brief presentation of several hitherto published theories of political economy of trade protection and their application on the case of agricultural protectionism.

## 1. The Political Economy of Protectionism

Protectionism can be generally defined as

> "policy of protecting domestic industries against foreign competition by means of tariffs, subsidies, import quotas, or other restrictions or handicaps placed on the imports of

---

[5] *Lima* (2012).
[6] See: http://epp.eurostat.ec.europa.eu/statistics_explained/index.php /Agricultural_labour_input (Accessed April 12, 2013).

*foreign competitors. Protectionist policies have been implemented by many countries despite the fact that virtually all mainstream economists agree that the world economy generally benefits from free trade*".[7]

One can wonder, why this is the case? Why if free trade is such a good thing[8], one can't see it in practice? The easiest answer to this question is: politics. The absence of free trade lies in the simple observation that the trade policy is not determined by those who try to maximize economic efficiency, but rather by those seeking for their own interests. Economic theory has failed to explain protectionism and that's why the economists have turned to the political factors to interpret the grounds of protectionist measures. When setting up the framework of political economy model one has to identify five main actors and the interactions among them. These are: individual citizens, firms, common interest groups, domestic government and foreign governments (along with various other foreign groups, such as international organizations and foreign private interest organizations). The preferences and the interplay between these actors determine country's international economic policy.[9]

In these political models the policy officials act always strategically and in own self-interest. Their decisions to put through the (agricultural) protectionist measures cause more costs than benefits to the society as whole. It's given that it's possible to affect the policy only at high costs. This prevents the "losers", tax payers who have to carry the costs, from striking for a reform of such a policy.[10]

According to Robert E. Baldwin (1996) the economist's grounds on which the political economy is based are substantial foundations in the microeconomics, as well as the behavior theory. Consequently the

---

[7]http://www.britannica.com/EBchecked/topic/479643/protectionism (Accessed April 12, 2013).

[8]The idea of advantages of free trade date back to Ricardo and even earlier. Classical models and variations of the Heckscher-Ohlin model document the fact that the capability of a country to partake in free trade enhances the country's benefits, such as production along the lines of comparative advantages and higher social utility. Further gains from trade come from specialization, economies of scale, improved quality and technology of production, and higher competition. To underline the main perks of transition from autarky to free trade, economists usually mention improved allocation of resources and increased welfare.

[9]*Baldwin* (1996).

[10]More onto this topic will be mention in the next subchapter.

functions of political markets are explained similarly as those of the economic markets. We assume rational individuals, preferences according to consumption and effort to maximize the welfare. Moreover individuals and firms are able to organize into common economic interest groups to demand certain kinds of protection. This protection is supplied by the public officials, who are considered to have their own economic self-interests. They look for reelection and therefore take the demands of individuals and firms into account. Obviously the firms or individuals who contribute more to the campaigns receive more attention from the government.

The theory which introduced the special interest groups and their influence on the trade policy of a country was the one by Grossman and Helpman (1994). Their basic model "protection for sale" started the research into the political economy of trade. In their framework they connected politics to economics in order to explain why one never sees free trade in practice. The reason for the protectionist measures is according to Grossman and Helpman the lobbying activity of interest groups in different industries. The trade policy function is considered to be a device transferring income to certain groups in society. Politically interesting groups are said to get more income thanks to the lobbying. The empirical study of Goldberg and Maggi (1999) proved that the trade protection is higher in the industries represented by a lobby.

One can conclude that the influence of the actors on the trade policy differs. It's said that the trade protection benefits only a small number of firms and workers whereas the majority of consumers lose out. Deviation from the free trade brings certainly some social costs. The financial gains from protection are acquired by the interest groups, who are politically influential, and the costs are spread among the consumers.

Even before GH model Lionel Robbins (1976) claimed that the classical economists were underestimating the power of producers and their ability to influence the economic policy of governments. The conclusion that can be drawn out of his studies is this one: any industry which gets the protection from the government would be of envy of other industries and these will therefore start looking for such protection too. Furthermore the protectionist measures are according to Lionel Robbins never applied only for a short time and there is a high probability of retaliation.

Stigler (1971) implied that the government is characterized by a political-support function which compares the gain in political support of those who are positively affected by the regulatory measures, and the loss in support of those who actually lose because of the regulations imposed.

Another question of high concern is why do citizens in advanced industrialized countries bear the high prices of subsidized products? One can wonder why they aren't lobbying against the protectionist tools, when it's clear that such measures "harm" their welfare and increase their costs. Several studies showed that the combined losses of the consumers top the gains of the producers, as to the agricultural protectionism. One explanation for the low organizational and lobbying ability of the consumers is the free-rider problem. If every consumer thinks his contribution won't change the protectionist policy, he will decide not to contribute, no matter whether other consumers do contribute or not. Thus at the end nobody opposes the protectionist policy (Prisoner's dilemma). Further explanations and the application of before mentioned theorems to the case of agriculture will be presented in the next subchapter.

## 2. The Political Economy of Agricultural Protectionism

In search for the answer to the problematic of persistence of agricultural protectionism, this subchapter will mention and analyze some explanations that have been offered in the literature of the political economy of agriculture.

To begin with, a classical reasoning can be found in the public choice studies. Theory of collective action by Olson (1965) could be the one to explain the "number paradox": why is a small specific interest group easier to organize and exert pressure than a large group of consumers. Olson stated that a small group with common interests and preferences is better able to organize itself, overcome the free rider problem[11] and collect the sources needed for effective lobbying. A group with homogeneous preferences can coordinate their actions more easily than group composed of different members with heterogeneous interests. There-

---

[11] Free-rider problem: There is possibility that some members may benefit from the group's action, without having to contribute to its costs. The larger the group, the easier it becomes for members to free-ride.

fore, a small group of farmers is definitely more efficient at lobbying than a large consumer group, considering the agricultural paradox.

Olson (1985) further applied these hypotheses to the problem of agricultural protectionism. He showed that despite the fact that agricultural producer groups differentiate one from another, they all have an interest in greater agricultural protection. In comparison the consumers and tax payers don't feel the urge to organize, even despite the fact that they all would beneficiate from protectionism 'reduction. A good explanation for the low organizational capacity of consumers in this particular case can be found in the "rational ignorance" theory: individuals, who lose merely a small amount per person by the protectionism imposed, will have only little incentive to invest to influence the policy.

> "If only those with large sums at stake are likely to pursue influence over policy, then the policies we see are likely to be ones whose benefits are concentrated among a few while the costs are spread among many."[12]

Total costs might be larger than total gains, but if the cost to each individual is low enough, consumers won't notice or care about those losses. Costs are spread widely and benefits are concentrated narrowly, to conclude, as in opposition to the situation in developing countries, as was before mentioned in the second chapter.[13]

Another explanation for the strong support of agriculture in developed countries can be found in the studies of Magee et al. (1989). The "sponsorship" to the farmers is attributed to the so-called "compensation effect". It states that the contributions of government go mostly to the sectors which lag behind or are for example suffering from economic crisis more than other sectors. The reason could lie in the ability of declining sector to pressure the government in times of adversity, as possible rewards from lobbying increase when the incomes from productive economic activities fall. Moreover, farmers are counting with possible benefits, as these might overcome the costs connected with lobbying activity. This is in accordance with the study of Bullock and

---

[12] *William A. Masters* in study of FAO: *The evolving structure of world agricultural trade: Implications for trade policy and trade agreements. Trends in agricultural protection: How might agricultural protection evolve in the coming decades?* 2009 p. 82.

[13] *Downs* (1957).

Coggins (2002), as mentioned by Weinberg and Bakker (2011). They found out that U.S. agricultural producers acquire larger rents in comparison with the efforts they have to put into lobbying. The "compensation effect" can be also applied to Common Agricultural Policy (CAP) of European Union, where farmers' incomes depend to a great extent on governmental supports. Political authorities have inclination to preserve the income of specific groups in society, in particular during periods of economic crisis. Hence, with the ongoing economic development, and decreasing role and size of agriculture, farmers rely on increasing state supports and governments try to maintain the standard of living of farmers.

Economic development can be further considered as the primary determinant of agriculture protection. Anderson and Hayami (1986) developed a function of agricultural protection according to the economic development of a country. In the initial stage of country's development agriculture is usually taxed while industrial sector is rather stimulated. When country reaches the next stage of development, agricultural producers start to lobby for governmental protection because their incomes lay behind workers employed in the industrial sector.

Weinberg and Bakker (2011) agreed that the development process highly affects the amount of protectionist measures used. They mentioned two main arguments to support this idea. First of all, agricultural sector needs motives to demand such protection and these motives come usually from abrupt decline of agriculture due to economic development of a country. Secondly, higher development means that consumers pay less for agricultural goods than before. With increasing income per capita, the relative share of expenditures on food declines, and therefore consumers become less sensitive to food prices. Relative costs will change, and the proportion of income spent on food declines even if actual expenditure on food rises (Engel's Law). Consequently, with increasing national income and decreasing volume of farmers, the resistance against the agricultural support diminishes, as was further investigated by Anderson and Tyers (1988) and Anderson (1991).[14]

Considering the consumers' resistance against the protectionist measures, there have been several theories published on how the citizens (consumers) hold the government responsible for their actions. The hypothesis of "reward-punishment" was applied to the voting be-

---

[14]Mentioned in *Weinberg and Bakker* (2011).

havior[15] as well as to the probability to start a revolution or social movement against the government. Weinberg and Bakker (2011) in their consumer based research in political economy of agricultural protectionism mentioned, that one can't underestimate the effect of consumer dissatisfaction over high prices, especially over high food prices. Since the protectionist rules increase the food prices for the consumers, this could provoke the citizens into opposing such policies, in order to make the costs decline. Important to mention, there has to be an actual cost associated with the protectionist policies to make the consumers willing to react and fight the policies. Besides that, the incomes of households and geographic location also play a great role at these "revolutionary" intentions. The events in the Middle East in recent years have shown the potential power of consumers to influence government decision-making to their benefit.[16] In comparison, there were several studies published on the issue of mass support of consumers for the agricultural protectionism in developed countries.[17] Very interesting interpretation of the consumer's behavior was presented in the work of Naoi and Kume (2011), who were trying to explain the support of the citizens for the agricultural protectionism. They conducted an experiment in 2008 in Japan and came with this result: the consumers have simply sympathy for "poor" and "hardworking" people, in this case farmers. Naoi and Kume further discovered that the general public projects their own job insecurity onto symbolic declining industry-agriculture. In sum, according to their experiment:

> "consumers appear to favor, rather than tolerate, agricultural protection."

Finally, this subchapter will end with mentioning several straightly political factors and their appraisal to the political economy of agriculture. Bilal (2000) presented a model in which the voting systems affect agricultural policies. He based his theory on outcomes made in public choice theory by Mueller (1989). According to Mueller, policy-making is a process of asymmetrical information, as voters never have complete information about the policies and gathering all the information is costly. The citizens will search for the information till the

---

[15] *Bilal* (2000).
[16] For further analysis of consumer-based approach review *Weinberg and Bakker* (2011).
[17] Further see Kindleberger: *"Theory of group behavior and international trade"* (1951).

marginal cost of doing so outweighs the marginal benefit of having such information.[18] Hence, voters behave rationally by staying partly uninformed and ignorant.[19] Bilal (2000) further applied this approach to the context of agriculture. He assumed that the voting models theory makes a good explanation for why voters don't make an effort to understand all the intrigues of agricultural policies. An attempt to collect all the information of policy-making of agricultural protectionism would be very costly for consumers and hence by staying "ignorant" to these policies, they act rationally. This may also explain the fact, why are some protectionist measures adopted by politicians highly ineffective: the governments simply don't fear losing their electorate, as they assume that the consumers are rather ignorant towards the effectiveness of protectionist measures applied.

Last factor that will be mentioned in this subchapter is the "restaurant bill problem" (or dinner check problem), which was applied by Bilal (2000) to the collective choice process and is considered to be relevant in the case of the European Union. The "restaurant bill problem" is based on a situation, where more people have a dinner together, and each person orders own meal, but the restaurant bill is then shared equally among all people sitting at the table. In such situation, each individual pays more, than he would have done otherwise, as human behavior leads some people to order more expensive meals, knowing that the costs will be shared and paid by many. According to Bilal (2000) this framework fits the participation of EU member states in the Common Agricultural Policy: despite the fact that a member state may not agree with the CAP, but it's forced to be included and pay for the common budget together with others, it prefers higher payments for its farmers (and other measures), than it would prefered otherwise. This naturally increases the costs of CAP and lead to support for an inefficient redistributive policy, since the states are "discharged" of the responsibility for their own agricultural budgets. This pattern may be true also for the negotiations at the international level. Considering agriculture, the discussions about agriculture were included as late as in the Uruguay Round of WTO, and before the URAA, agriculture was more or less completely omitted from the GATT, even despite the fact that inclusion of agricultural talks might have been beneficial for a great number of trading partners. According to Bilal (2000) agree-

---

[18] Further see Mueller: *Public choice II.* (1989).
[19] Further see Downs: *An economic theory of democracy* (1957).

ments during the Uruguay Round (UR) were a result of "restaurant bill" situations, what the exclusions and derogations for agricultural measures or goods concerns. Further analysis of the WTO negotiations and problematic of EU' Common Agricultural Policy will be mentioned in the next chapter.

## IV. Agricultural Protectionism in Western World

The economists have been warning of heavy governmental interventions in trade throughout the world for past decades. Short analysis of the large variety of theories, that has been published in order to explain the persistence of (agricultural) protectionism, was provided in the last chapter. Despite all the published studies, the arguments of economists haven't been in most cases conceived and the political factors keep predominating the agricultural policy setting and trade policy in both developed and developing countries. The disputes about the agricultural policy play major role in international trade relations, as can be observed by the struggles over Doha Round of multilateral trade negotiations.

In the last chapter of this work a brief analysis of current situation of agricultural protectionism in western world will be provided. The focus here will be mainly on two relevant issues: the Common Agricultural Policy of European Union and Doha Development Round of WTO. Since the extant of the paper is limited, the problematic will be only shortly outlined, and several questions, that require further investigation, will be raised.

### 1. The EU and Agricultural Protectionism

The European Union (EU) is often perceived as a good example for regional integration[20] and encouragement of trade between its members and other trade partners. The EU managed to reduce many trade barriers and even lowered its tariffs on industrial imports to the lowest rate among WTO member states. Although the EU promotes free trade throughout the world, it still protects its key industry sectors; the best

---

[20] As the members of the EU created a customs union and removed all the tariffs with respect to each other.

known example of EU' protectionism includes its Common Agricultural Policy (CAP).

The CAP was set up during the formation of the European Economic Community (EEC) and since then turned into massive export subsidy program. The CAP can be described as an agricultural policy that enforces trade barriers on agricultural products from abroad, and at the same time provides subventions to domestic farmers. However, CAP didn't start as an export subsidy program, but as an attempt to guarantee high prices to European agricultural producers. Nevertheless this policy-decision resulted in huge food overproduction in the EU. To get rid of the major food storages, subsidizing export became necessary. Despite the fact that the EU has a comparative disadvantage in agricultural production and would be actually an importer of food under free trade, the great level of subsidies and guarantees for high prices have turned it into a food exporter. Yet export subsidies are technically illegal under the WTO, powerful lobbying in the U.S., EU and other developed countries ensured that they are allowed in the agricultural sector.[21]

What is also alarming is the proportion of costs and benefits of agricultural protectionism. In 2011 the average share of agriculture to the GDP in the member states of European Union was around 1-2%[22], while the CAP absorbed 44% of the entire EU budget.[23] While European farmers benefit from large subsidization, as it provides them with higher income and job security, the consumers suffer in a large extent, as they have to pay significantly higher prices for food and even higher taxes for the subsidization. Moreover, the share of agricultural labor force in EU is only around 5%.[24] Yet this relatively small group of farmers appears to be well-organized, as they have been very successful in pushing through their interests.[25] The promoters and defenders of the Common Agricultural Policy claim that such policy is needed, as it helps to decrease the reliance on foreign food import and increase the self-sufficiency and agricultural employment and even supports the

---

[21] *Krugman and Obstfeld* (2009).

[22] http://data.worldbank.org/indicator/NV.AGR.TOTL.ZS (Accessed April 15, 2013).

[23] http://ec.europa.eu/agriculture/cap-post-2013/graphs/graph1_en.pdf (Accessed April 15, 2013).

[24] http://epp.eurostat.ec.europa.eu/statistics_explained/index.php/Agricultural_labour_input (Accessed April 15, 2013).

[25] To review the theoretical explanations for lobbying see the third chapter.

survival of rural citizenry. In fact, if Europe tried to remove its trade barriers and subsidization program, the entire agricultural sector would be possibly driven out of business. Nevertheless, this argument is too weak to defend the massive CAP spending.

In response to all the criticism, the EU introduced some reforms of CAP in 2003[26] and announced that the CAP needs to undergo some radical rebuilding. The innovations that were presented include the "decoupling" of income support payments to farmers from quantity of production, with lower guaranteed prices and a new rural development policy built on food safety and environmentally friendly practices.[27] In recent years EU propagates the multifunctional role of AP, with variety of objectives, while claiming that the agriculture is a sector which needs "special treatment". The important question here is, whether these promoted reforms aren't just a justification for increasing protectionism. The further reforms, embracing substantial cuts of export subsidies and import duties are still currently being discussed between the member states.[28] The EU nevertheless asserts that the negotiations on CAP between member states will continue, even if the talks at the Doha Round aren't successful, and it is certain, that this debate won't end anytime soon.

## 2. The WTO Doha Round of Trade Negotiations

The World Trade Organization (WTO) supervises and regulates trade and tariffs worldwide and attempts to liberalize the international commerce. The cornerstone of WTO and of its predecessor GATT (General Agreement on Tariffs and Trade) as well, is the neoclassical economic theory, founded on the principles of specialization and comparative advantages. It states that the trade is always mutually beneficial and superior to protectionism, as protectionism isn't effective and conductive towards the world welfare. Protectionism is the result of the internal negotiating process, which includes policy makers and lobbyists, plus producers and consumers. Nevertheless the protectionist tools clash with the internal (consumers) and external (WTO) barriers. Consid-

---

[26] For more data see: http://europa.eu/legislation_summaries/agriculture/general_framework/160002_en.htm.

[27] http://ec.europa.eu/agriculture/cap-history/2003-reform/index_en.htm (Accessed April 15, 2013).

[28] http://www.europeanvoice.com/article/2013/march/farm-ministers-agree-common-position-on-cap-reform/76700.aspx (Accessed April 15, 2013).

ering the external barriers to protectionism, one can say that the rules of WTO originated to justify rejection of protectionism.

The last but one Round of WTO negotiations has finally brought agriculture within the WTO platform, which happened after 47 years of establishment of GATT. The Uruguay Round Agreement on Agriculture (URAA) in 1994 is therefore considered as a major achievement in regard to trade with agricultural products. It has also raised public attention to the agricultural interventions and started a discussion about the desirability and effectiveness of protectionist measures used. As protectionism in agriculture worldwide remains higher than in other sectors of economy, it's clear that the current Doha Round of WTO negotiations on agriculture deserve the top priority. Nevertheless it also makes the reaching of common agreement harder. "Current" negotiations should bring a continuation of liberalization process as defined by the URAA. The objective defined in the Doha Ministerial Declaration in 2001 was recalled and referred to the Agreement and it is

> *"to establish a fair and market-oriented trading system through a programme of fundamental reform encompassing strengthened rules and specific commitments on support and protection in order to correct and prevent restrictions and distortions in world agricultural markets. . . ".*

Needless to say, agricultural policies of member states of WTO are determined by the reforms passed by the organization. It's of general knowledge that the EU's reforms of CAP over the past two decades were stimulated by the progress and coincided with the reforms introduced by the GATT/WTO negotiations.[29] The effects of government interventions are subject to the level of chosen support and also to the selection of the instrument of agricultural policy. These instruments are classified by WTO into three categories: green, blue and amber boxes, according to their distorting effects and consequences on production and trade.[30]

Swinnen, Olper and Vandermoortele (2011) published a study on policy instrument choice in agricultural policies. They examined the impact of the WTO on agricultural and food policies and came out with interesting results: the GATT/WTO rules have not reduced total

---

[29] *Anderson* (2010).

[30] For further explanation see: http://www.wto.org/english/tratop_e/agric_e/agboxes_e.htm.

amount of subsidies to farmers used by various countries, but they put effective constraint on the use of distortionary agricultural policies. Meaning, the URAA brought usage of less distortionary measures, even though it didn't significantly affect the total amount of the support to the farmers.[31]

Nonetheless the remaining distortions on the agricultural markets are still huge and it's obvious that they are responsible for a great amount of the global welfare' cost, even though agriculture accounts only for 3-4% of global GDP. Generally, the liberalization of agricultural trade would improve global economic welfare. This is the reason why the negotiations of Doha Round have to continue. Alarming is still the fact, that they have started in 2001 and there haven't been any relevant conclusion ever since. Apparently, the agricultural sector stays in a special concern of many countries and as was proven before, and the protectionist interventions are easier to be implemented, than to be subsequently removed. Whether the negotiators achieve the projected goal of cuts in subsidies, tariffs etc. set forth in the Doha Round of WTO, still remains an open question.

# V. Conclusion

The aim of this work was to discuss controversial topic of persistence of agricultural protectionism in the western world. In doing so, the paper provided a brief overview of the most relevant theories of political economy and their application to the case of agricultural trade policies, primarily to the agricultural protectionism. Moreover, brief evidence of protectionist measures of the Common Agricultural Policy of the European Union was mentioned, as well as the importance of the WTO negotiations related to the issue of agricultural trade.

To start with summarizing of the topic, it's crucial to remark that the agriculture still remains the most distortive sector of the world trade, even despite the fact that its contribution to the global GDP is the lowest of all sectors. It has been said, that the agricultural trade barriers and producer subsidies affect negatively countries' economies, as they inflict the real costs, induce oversupply by supporting inefficient producers, hurt exporters from developing countries and generally negatively affect international food prices, mainly by raising their level for

---

[31] Nevertheless this effect was stronger for the OECD members.

the consumers. When looking at the case of European Common Agricultural Policy, particularly at the massive export subsidy program, we see that the costs of this policy clearly outweigh the benefits to the society as whole. The benefits as job stability and higher income for producers are of advantage only to a small number of farmers, as these make only little share of the whole labor force and the costs are spread among a large number of consumers (in the developed countries). There were several explanations for this "anomaly" discussed in the paper. First of all, the significant lobbying force of the farmers was referred to and explained in the text from the standpoint of different theories of political economy. Secondly, when looking at the problematic from the point of view of consumers, who have to bear the higher costs, there were various interpretations for their behavior mentioned in the text: the rational ignorance theory, Prisoner's dilemma and also the sympathy for producers and projection of consumers own job insecurity on the support for farmers.

We will finish with the question, related to the "development paradox", which was raised at the beginning of the paper and that is: why do the developed countries subsidize and the developing countries tax their agricultural sector. We may not find the relevant answer yet, nevertheless it's of high concern, whether the developing and later industrialized countries will copy the current policies of advanced high-income countries, and subsequently try to protect their agricultural sector by high subsidization themselves. For this reason, the multilateral negotiations of WTO and the successful conclusion of the Doha Development Round are necessary.

# Reference

Printed Sources:

*Anderson, Kym* (1991), *Lobbying Incentives and Pattern of Protection in Rich and Poor Countries.* Geneva: GATT Secretariat.

*Anderson, Kym* (2010), Agricultural Policies: Past, Present and Prospective under Doha. In: *World Trade Institute's book on The End of Cheap Food and the WTO,* edited by Baris Karapinar and Christian Häberli. Cambridge University Press.

*Anderson, Kym, and Hayami, Yujiro* (1986), *The Political Economy of Agricultural Protection: East Asia in International Perspective.* London: Allen and Unwin.

*Anderson, Kym and Tyers R.* (1988), The Pattern of Distortions to Agricultural Incentives. In: *Agriculture and Governments in an Interdependent World,* eds. Maunder, Allen and Alberto Valdes. Darthmounth: Aldershot, pp. 175-186.

*Baldwin, Robert E.* (1996), The Political Economy of Trade Policy: Integrating the Perspectives of Economists and Political Scientists. In: *The Political Economy of Trade Policy,* eds. Feenstra, Robert C., Grossman, Gene M., and Irwin, Douglas A. The MIT Press. Cambridge (Mass), London, pp. 147-174.

*Bilal, Sanoussi* (2000), The Political Economy of Agricultural Policies and Negotiations. In: *Negotiating the Future of Agricultural Policies: Agricultural Trade and the Millennium WTO Round,* eds. Sanoussi Bilal and Pavlos Pezaros. The Hague: Kluwer Law International, pp. 81-93.

*Bullock, David S., and Coggins, Jay S.* (2002), Do Farmers Receive Huge Rents for Small Lobbying Efforts? In: *Agricultural Policy for the 21st Century,* eds. Luther Tweeten and Stanley R. Thompson. Ames: Iowa State University Press, pp. 146-59.

*Downs, Anthony* (1957), *An economic theory of democracy.* New York: Harper & Row.

*Goldberg, Pinelopi K. and Maggi, Giovanni* (1999), Protection for Sale: An Empirical Investigation. In: *American Economic Review*, Volume 89, Issue 5, pp. 1135-1155.

*Grossman, Gene and Helpman, Elhanan* (1994), Protection for Sale. In: *American Economic Review*, 84 (4), pp. 833-50.

*Kindleberger, Charles P.* (1951), Group behaviour and international trade.In: *Journal of Political Economy*, Volume 59, No. 1

*Krugman, Paul R. and Obstfeld Maurice* (2009), *International Economics: Theory and Policy*. Pearson International Edition, 8$^{th}$ edition.

*Lima, Thiago* (2012), Agricultural protectionism in developed countries as a State interest. In: *Brazilian Journal of International Relations*. Edicao Quadrimestral, Volume 1.

*Magee, Stephen P., Brock, William A. and Young, Leslie* (1989), *Black Hole Tariffs and Endogenous Policy Theory: Political Economy in General Equilibrium*. Cambridge: Cambridge University Press.

*Masters, Williams* (2009), Trends in Agricultural Protection: How Might Agricultural Policy Evolve in the Coming Decades? In: *The Evolving Structure of World Agricultural Trade*, eds. Alexander Sarris and Jamie Morrison. Rome, Italy: FAO, 2009, pp. 79-108.

*Mueller, Dennis C.* (1989), *Public choice II*. Cambridge: Cambridge University Press.

*Naoi, Megumi and Kume, Ikuo* (2011), Explaining Mass Support for Agricultural Protectionism: Evidence from a Survey Experiment During the Global Recession. In: *International Organization*, Volume 65, No. 4, pp. 771-795.

*Olson, Mancur* (1965), *The Logic of Collective Action: Public Goods and the Theory of Groups*. Cambridge, MA: Harvard University Press.

*Olson, Mancur* (1985), The Exploitation and Subsidization of Agriculture in Developing and Developed Countries; In: *Agriculture in a Turbulent World Economy*, eds. Allen Maunder and Ulf Renborg. Aldershot, England: Gower, pp. 49-59.

*Robbins, Lionel C.* (1976), *Political Economy, Past and Present*. New York, NY: Columbia University Press.

*Stigler, George J.* (1971), Theory of economic regulation. In: *Bell Journal of Economics*, (2), pp. 13-29.

Swinnen, J.F.M., Olper, A. and Vandemoortele, T. (2011), Impact of the WTO on Agricultural and Food Policies. In: *The World Economy*, 35(9), pp. 1089-1101.

Thies, Cameron G. and Porche, Schuyler (2007), The Political Economy of Agricultural Protection; In: *The Journal of Politics*, Volume 69, No. 1, pp. 116-127.

Timmer, C. P. (Ed.) (1991), *Agriculture and the state: Growth, employment, and poverty in developing countries*. Ithaca. NY: Cornell University Press.

Weinberg, Joe and Bakker, Ryan (2012), Betting the farm on high food prices: A consumer based approach to agriculture protection. In: *The Social Science Journal*, Volume 49, pp. 191-201.

Internet Sources:

Encyclopedia Britannica. http://www.britannica.com/.
European Commission. Eurostat Homepage. http://epp.eurostat.ec.europa.eu/portal/page/portal/eurostat/home/.
European Commission. CAP expenditure – European Commission, DG Agriculture and Rural Development (Financial Reports); EU expenditure – European Commission, DG Budget (2009 Financial report). Annual expenditure, in 2007 constant prices. http://ec.europa.eu/agriculture/cap-post2013/graphs/graph1_en.pdf [accessed on 15.04.2013].
European Commission. Eurostat (2010), Agricultural labor input. Data from May 2010. http://epp.eurostat.ec.europa.eu/statistics_explained/index.php/Agricultural_labour_input [accessed on 15.04.2013].
European Commission. Agriculture and Rural Development. History of the CAP (2012). The 2003 reform. http://ec.europa.eu/agriculture/cap-history/2003-reform/index_en.htm [accessed on 15.04.2013].
Europa: European Union Website (2013), Reform of the common agricultural policy (CAP). http://europa.eu/legislation_summaries/agriculture/general_framework/l60002_en.htm [accessed on 15.04.2013].

*Keating, Dave* (2013), Farm ministers agree common position on CAP reform. European Voice 20.03.2013. http://www.europeanvoice.com/article/2013/march/farm-ministers-agree-common-position-on-cap-reform/76700.aspx [accessed on 15.04.2013].

The World Bank Data (2013), Agriculture, value added (% of GDP). http://data.worldbank.org/indicator/NV.AGR.TOTL.ZS [accessed on 15.04.2013].